Plan On Purpose
GUIDEBOOK

*An instrument to help you discern
and live your life purpose*

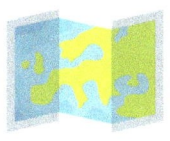 

THIS GUIDEBOOK BELONGS TO:

_____

START DATE OF PLAN:

_____

- with GREGG HANSCOM
CEO (Creator, Encourager, Optimist)
Hanscom Creative, LLC
www.HanscomCreative.com

Edited by Lil Barcaski

Published by: GWN Publishing
www.GWNPublishing.com

ISBN: 978-1-959608-93-6

Dedication

Dedicated to everyone who has been lost, is lost, may become lost or lost again, or is in fear of never being found. God loves you.

Jeremiah 29:11-13

"For I know the plans I have for you," declares the Lord, "plans for welfare and not for evil, to give you a future and a hope. Then you will call upon me and come and pray to me, and I will hear you. You will seek me and find me, when you seek me with all your heart."

Plan On Purpose

The *Plan On Purpose Guidebook* to accompany *Donkey's Purpose* story, or to use as a separate tool for all ages to discern and live your life's purpose.

This *Plan On Purpose Guidebook* is:

- Your PLAN, ON your PURPOSE: map and compass to explore and navigate

- Your PLAN, ON PURPOSE: innovate, not waiting for fate, or something to happen

- Your action to PLAN, ON your PURPOSE: innovate and navigate, intentionally and deliberately

- Your action to PLAN ON PURPOSE: to explore, innovate, navigate, and activate, according to God's will for you, not by accident, nor by chance.

Each prompt question has a space partly lined for writing answers or thoughts, and an open space for free-writing, jotting-down, doodle, sketch, add pictures, calculations, etc.

If a picture says 1,000 words, and you are only writing ideas, you are at less than full capacity for your creativity! Also, if you are only taking digital notes on your phone or computer, you are limiting your creativity without the freedom to sketch and doodle additional ideas!

It is also okay to color outside the lines, and create outside the box! Use additional sheets of paper, then staple them to the appropriate page to keep all of your ideas in one place in this Guidebook!

If you're working with a group, I recommend you pass your pages around to get others' thoughts and ideas!

For example, let's say your youth group needs to come up with some plans and ideas to increase attendance and participation, or your sales team needs to come up with some plans and ideas for a new product roll-out...

- Each person writes an idea down and passes their sheet to the left.

- Each person reads the idea at the top of the new sheet; it sparks a thought about another related idea that might improve upon the previous ideas on the page; write it down, and pass the sheet to the left.

- Continue passing and writing until everybody has their own sheet again with a list of ideas, one from each person in the group.

- Discuss all the ideas and choose the top two or three ideas and prioritize how to implement one immediately, and set goals to complete others.

(Individuals also use this method to write as many ideas as possible!)

Orienteering

ORIENTEERING: (noun) a competitive or noncompetitive recreational activity in which participants use a map and compass to navigate between checkpoints along an unfamiliar course (as in the woods).[1]

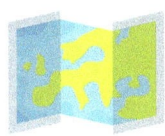 A MAP shows the land, but it is not as useful if you do not know where you are, do not know the destination, and do not know which direction to travel.

 A COMPASS shows direction to magnetic north, but is not as useful if you do not know where you are, or do not know the destination.

Used together, you can properly orient the map according to true north by calculating the angle of declination from the needle pointing to magnetic north, and reach any destination on the map.

1. Always believe your compass!

2. Know that it is appropriate to also ask for directions to be sure you are traveling toward your destination!

---

1   *Merriam-Webster Dictionary*

PLAN ON PURPOSE

Identify & Discern God's Calling for You!

Define your life purpose

Clarify your life purpose

Identify goals based on your life purpose

Set your intentions

Plan your work, then work your plan

Then you will be living your life on purpose!

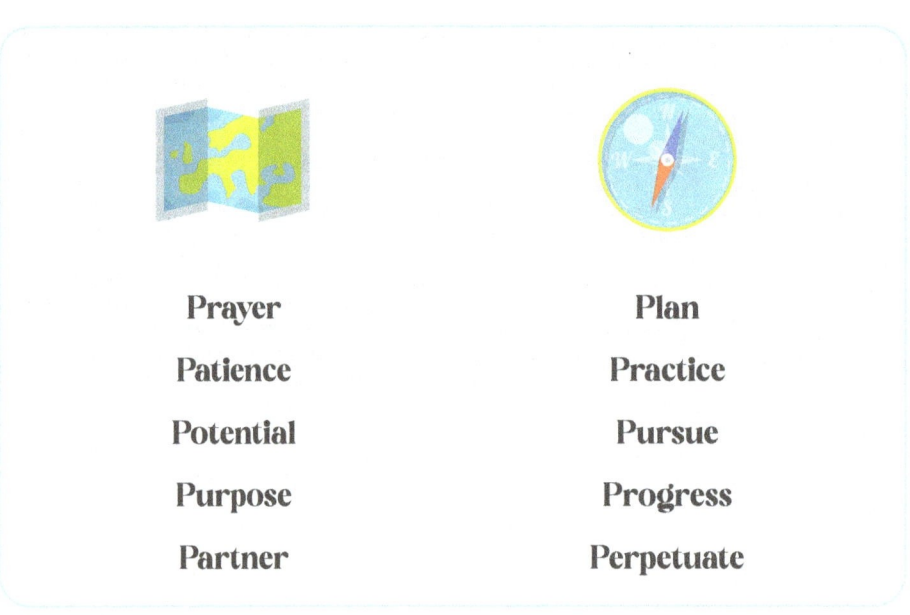

Prayer	Plan
Patience	Practice
Potential	Pursue
Purpose	Progress
Partner	Perpetuate

Now you are ready to begin to discern God's purpose for you!

Walk in a manner worthy of the Lord, and live your life on purpose!

Begin with reading Bible verses for Inspiration (also great for group discussions):

- Psalm 139:16
- Ephesians 1:11
- Jeremiah 1:4-8
- Proverbs 22:29
- 1 Corinthians 12:1-11
- Ephesians 2:10
- Exodus 35:10
- James 1:17
- 1 Peter 4:10-11
- Exodus 31:3-5
- Matthew 6:1-4
- Romans 12:3-8

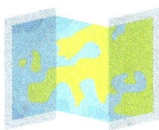

maP — *Prayer, Patience, Potential, Purpose, Partner*

The first five P's are the map; the big picture to determine:

- where you are now

- where you are going

- what is the path to travel

comPass — *Plan, Practice, Pursue, Progress, Perpetuate*

The last five P's are the compass; always pointing magnetic north, and when used with the map (true North) and adjusted for the magnetic declination:

- how to reach your destination

- set the bearing or azimuth to determine direction to travel, 0-360 degrees

- what distance to travel

- when you will arrive

Prayer

Matthew 6:7–8*

And when you pray, do not heap up empty phrases as the Gentiles do, for they think they will be heard for their many words. Do not be like them, for your Father knows what you need before you ask him.

Ephesians 2:10*

For we are His workmanship, created in Christ Jesus for good works, which God prepared beforehand that we should walk in them.

Colossians 1:10*

...so as to walk in a manner worthy of the Lord, fully pleasing to Him: bearing fruit in every good work and increasing in the knowledge of God...

Bible Gateway App

Patience

Empathy ▪ Hear God's Whispers ▪ God's Timing ▪ Misunderstand
Calling ▪ Your Wishes vs God's Will ▪ Patience Is Not Inaction

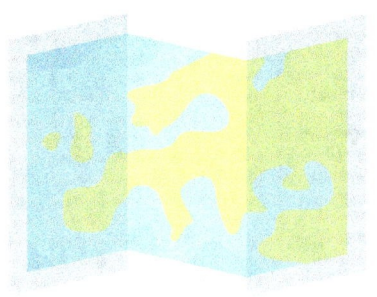

Potential

Explore: Your Abilities, Gifts and Talents ■ What Are You Good At? ■
What Do You Love To Do?

Purpose

Innovate ■ Why Are You Here On This Earth? ■ To Serve, Do God's Will, Experience Joy, Satisfaction ■ Success, & Happiness (20 ideas, possibilities!)

Partner

Empathy ■ Tell Someone About Your Intentions ■ Know Where You Are To Be If You Go Off Course ■ Hold You Accountable, Support, Guide ■ Hire A Coach

Plan

Explore ▪ Map-out ▪ Set Goals For Each Task Toward Your Purpose:
Start Date, Detailed, Trackable, Realistic, Pertinent, End Date

Practice

Navigate ■ Continual Prayer ■ Work Your Goals For Each Task ■
What Do You Need To Research, Learn, Experience, Improve?

Pursue

Activate ■ Take Action On Plan & Practice ■ Focus ■
Schedule, Prioritize, Re-Evaluate, Re-Set

Progress

Activate ■ One Day At A Time ■ Continue Forward With Confidence ■ According to Plan and Goals ■ Seek To Be A Blessing ■ Walk Worthy

Perpetuate

Pray ■ Listen For God's Will ■ Re-Assess Goals ■ Adjust Goals ■ Set New Goals ■ Repeat: Explore, Empathize, Innovate, Navigate, Activate

Deepen your understanding

These questions can help you deepen your understanding of your purpose and inspire you to take meaningful action towards fulfilling it:

1. What brings me the most fulfillment and joy in life?

2. What unique talents or skills do I possess?

3. How can I use my talents to serve others and make a positive impact?

1. What values are most important to me, and how do they align with my actions?

5. What activities or endeavors make me feel most alive and engaged?

6. What legacy do I want to leave behind?

7. How can I contribute to my community or society in a meaningful way?

8. What challenges or problems do I feel passionate about addressing?

9. What kind of person do I aspire to be, and what steps can I take to embody those qualities?

10. How can I align my daily actions with my long-term vision and purpose?

Clarify your life purpose

When you align with your purpose, then people, resources, and opportunities will naturally gravitate towards you. When you use your gifts and talents to serve others, then you are fulfilling your purpose. *Clarify your life purpose!*

SETTING MY INTENTIONS:

1. What **potential** do I envision within myself to *expand* and **progress** to make a more significant impact?

2. What *beliefs* do I need to adopt to **pursue** the actions or pathway that will enable me to embrace my **potential**?

3. What is the *single most impactful action* I can take to **pursue** completing my **plan**?

1. What would **I pursue** if *success was guaranteed*?

5. **What *motivates* me to take action?**

6. What is the *first step* I need to take?

7. What *result or impact* do I want to achieve?

8. What action lies *just beyond* my comfort zone?

9. What action is *far* outside my comfort zone?

_____

_____

_____

_____

_____

_____

_____

_____

_____

10. What will *boost* my chances of success?

II. What will be *simple*?

12. What will be *challenging*?

13. What will help me stay *focused*?

14. What *allies* or *collaborators* do I desire?

15. **What *resources* do I have access to?**

10. How will I *recognize* when I've reached my goal and succeeded?

17. **What outcome would *exceed my expectations*?**

Clarify Your Life Purpose!

It is crucial for each of us to understand the correlation between embracing our potential and fulfilling our purpose.

EXAMPLE:

*"My life purpose is to use my **humor, insights,** and **observations** to **encourage and inspire** others by providing them **hope and optimism** to be **joyful and caring** people who **encourage** their peers as they **pursue** their own **life purpose**."*

- GREGG HANSCOM
CEO (Creator, Encourager, Optimist)
Hanscom Creative, LLC

GIFTS & TALENTS: Humorous, funny, witty, observant, thoughtful, encouraging, inspiring, creative, knowledgeable, artistic, athletic, outdoorsman, sportsman, traveler, spiritual, writer, artist, HR Professional, parent, youth leader, mentor, trainer, organized, coach, musical, craftsman, handyman, hiker, biker, canoeist, kayaker, camper, swimmer, runner, unicycle, juggle, gardener of flowers and vegetables, church camp director, youth group, scout leader, merit badge counselor...

ACTION: Coach, mentor, inspire, encourage, positive, optimists, create, teach, lead by example, invent, design, build, write, paint, draw, serve, help, speak, present, communicate...

RESULT: Help people, train, present, teach, lead by example, organize, instruct, goal setting, based on purpose...

Clarify your life purpose!

GIFTS & TALENTS:

ACTION:

RESULT:

Write your life purpose!

MY LIFE PURPOSE IS TO:

Set Your Goal!

Based on your life purpose to make it pertinent:

Map-out, Set Goals For Each Task Toward Your Purpose; Start Date, Detailed, Trackable, Realistic, Pertinent, End Date

EXAMPLE:

*"Starting August 1, 2023, I will **write and illustrate a 20-page children's picture book about life purpose,** writing and drawing 4-pages per month by November 30, 2023, contract with a publisher by February 1, 2024 and **publish by April 1, 2024.***

- GREGG HANSCOM
CEO (Creator, Encourager, Optimist)
Hanscom Creative, LLC

AUTHOR'S NOTE: I re-assessed my plan in February as I had not yet contracted with a publisher, and adjusted my goals and continued to pursue... I contracted with GWN Publishing on May 14, 2024, established Hanscom Creative LLC the same day, and published this unexpected *Plan On Purpose Guide Book* on June 30, 2024, and published *Donkey's Purpose* on July 30, 2024.

Set your first goal toward living your life on purpose!

Using your answers in the previous pages of this guidebook... Start Date, Detailed, Trackable, Realistic, Pertinent, End Date

PERTINENT GOAL *(related to my life purpose)*:

STARTING DATE:

I WILL:

THIS IS HOW:

ENDING DATE:

Next Step

Now pray, and get started!

Once you succeed, do it again with another goal!

Please post your life purpose and a goal you completed! @HanscomCreative

Dear God, Please allow me to be a blessing to someone today and tomorrow. Thank you for bringing someone into my life to serve in Your name! Guide my thoughts, words, and actions as I answer Your call to carry out Your will for me. Amen

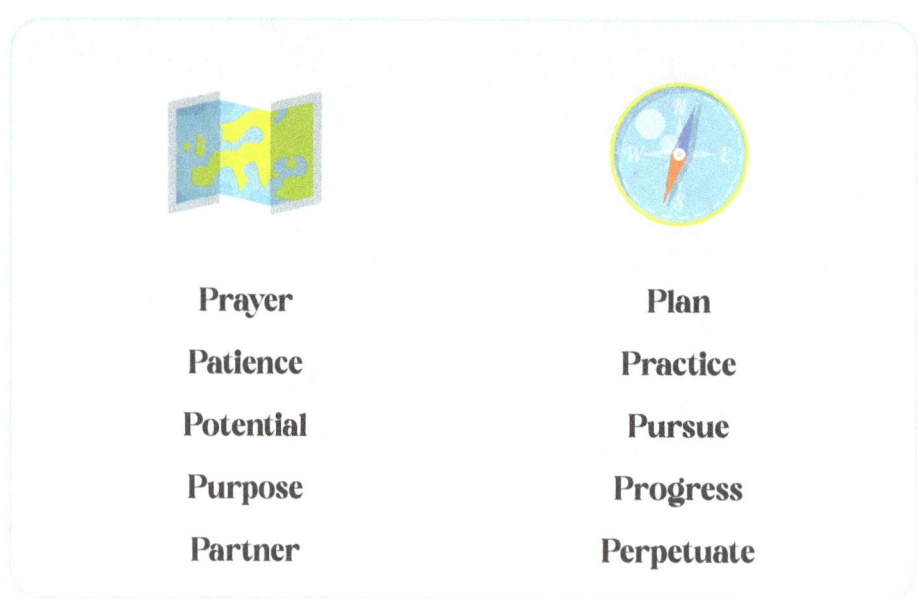

Prayer	Plan
Patience	Practice
Potential	Pursue
Purpose	Progress
Partner	Perpetuate

REFERENCE: This guidebook is based on concepts written in *The Success Principles* by Jack Canfield, as taught by my Coach Jean M. LaCour of NET Institute in her Coaching Certification Course, including *Q? Basics Coaching Mastery* by Marcy Nelson-Garrison, which all led me to setting my goals to write and publish *Donkey's Purpose*, and this unexpected *Plan On Purpose Guidebook*!

May God bless every person who uses this guidebook.

About the Author

GREGG HANSCOM is a Mental Fitness Coach, HR Leader, Church Camp Co-Director, and lover of nature, adventure, and living generational & genealogical history. Gregg lives in Maine near the restful mountains, and in Massachusetts near the restless ocean. He can be found; in the pursuit of happiness hiking & biking & running trails, kayaking & canoeing on ocean, lakes and rivers, and camping on "an explore", everywhere possible in God's creation; although he is no longer lost, and now living his life on purpose.

- GREGG HANSCOM, CEO
(Creator, Encourager, Optimist)
Hanscom Creative, LLC
www.HanscomCreative.com
@HanscomCreative social media

Also available from Hanscom Creative: "Donkey's Purpose" children's book; three biblical stories told from the donkey's perspective about their own life purpose.

Please post your successes and goals achieved while using the Plan On Purpose Guidebook! Walk in a manner worthy of the Lord, and live your life on purpose!

Purpose of This Guidebook

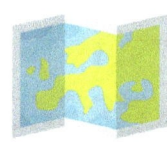 

This Plan On Purpose Guidebook is an instrument to help you discern and live your life's purpose. Walk in a manner worthy of the Lord, and live your life on purpose!

PLAN ON PURPOSE FOR:

- Individuals
- Families
- Friends
- Book Clubs
- Youth Groups
- Sunday Schools
- Vacation Bible Schools
- Summer Camps

- Church Camps
- Homeschools
- Youth Troops
- Christian Schools, Colleges & Universities
- Adult groups
- Bible Study

...AND GOD WILLING, USE FOR:

- Businesses
- Employers
- Non-profit Organizations
- Some public classrooms that allow God to dwell within their education institution communities
- Local, state, federal, national entities funded by tax-payers with foundations and statements based on God (USA examples):
- "In God We Trust"
- "One Nation Under God"

- "God shed His Grace on thee"
- "Nature's God"
- "I do solemnly swear, so help me God"
- "With a firm reliance on the protection of divine Providence, we mutually pledge to each other our Lives, our Fortunes and our sacred Honor."
- "We hold these truths to be self-evident, that all men are created equal, that they are endowed by their Creator with certain unalienable Rights, that among these are Life, Liberty and the pursuit of Happiness."